THE PSYCHOLOGY OF IGNORANCE

The Conflicted Mind in the Post-Truth World

———

The truth about Knowledge: it is ALWAYS finite
The truth about Ignorance: it is ALWAYS infinite

———

How understanding Ignorance
saves us from stupidity

JOHN VAN DIXHORN, PHD

In gratitude of:

The learning I received from a lifetime of patients who found a better life confronting their own ignorance as I was confronting mine.

My wife, Jana Holmer, whose ferocious reading and in depth interest in social issues along with her keen intelligence and innate goodness formed many of our daily exchanges that created this book.

Contents

INTRODUCTION

I CAN SEE this book being useful as a guide for discussion in a book group focused either on political or social topics or on developing deeper self-knowledge by recognizing conflicts between reason and ignorance in ourselves.

I felt that the strongest emotions came through in the sections treating the role of ignorance in its different forms, as a threat to sociopolitical relations in general and American democracy specifically.

All of us are struggling to deal with the social and psychological reality of "post-truth." The author's thoughts contribute to this discussion.

I found the most engaging examples were from the author's experience in sports.

Sarah Sarkissian, Retired English professor, and language specialist.

———⚮———

Not long after Donald Trump assumed the Presidency, the venerable Washington Post launched two initiatives. The paper adopted a new slogan which was added to its identifying masthead: Democracy Dies in Darkness. At roughly the same time, the paper also began charting – and printing – a running catalog of verifiable lies told by the President. That catalog eventually totaled some 38,000 demonstrable fabrications (on average, more than 25 lies every day the man held office).

Those two initiatives, celebrating facts as an essential tool of participatory democracy and exposing falsehoods as a means of countering the lies spewing from the White House, were at once noble and practical. Neither, however, had any impact at all on the most astonishing feature of the Trump era – nearly half the nation, those who voted for and vigorously supported Donald Trump, simply didn't care.

Pundits, politicians, talk show hosts, commentators and comics have all spent time, talent and energy – and it seems fair to note, entirely too many words – excoriating the strange and dystopian relationship Donald Trump has with reality. None, however, have approached that relationship very effectively; virtually all have failed to find the answer to the most perplexing facet of the Trump era (an era which, one notes, is not certainly over yet): How is it possible that so many embraced, celebrated and adopted the absurd notion that lies are truth and fiction is fact?

John Van Dixhorn, in clear, concise, and remarkably well-informed fashion, provides an answer. The Psychology of Ignorance examines the ways in which our brains can – and often do – allow us to make remarkably bad decisions by making what we believe to be remarkably good choices. In his brief but incisive analysis, Van Dixhorn provides the framework with which we analyze ignorance. We make irrational choices for rational reasons, we allow desires to shove reality out of the way, we think what we wish to think when it suits our needs – we shun uncomfortable truth to justify comforting ignorance.

Only when we understand our ignorance, Van Dixhorn insists, can we restore rationality and plain old common sense to our political universe.

It is not an exaggeration to suggest that the restoration of democracy – the banishment of darkness – can and will occur only if and when Van Dixhorn's approach is required reading in our classrooms, debates, discussions and, most of all, in any place where our elected officials – every last one of them – gather.

David M Hamlin, Author

CHAPTER 1

UNHEALTHY IGNORANCE VERSUS HEALTHY IGNORANCE

It's 369 B.C. and a thoughtful young thirty year old Greek guy named Socrates is disturbed, scratching his head in bewilderment. He just heard that The Oracle of Delphi, the revealed word of the gods, declared him the wisest man alive. This lands on him as ridiculous for he knows that's impossible, he certainly is not the wisest man alive. How can he still believe in the gods if they be so wrong?

He sets out to prove his point. He meets with astronomers who know so much about the cosmos than he does. He has the same experience meeting with the mathematicians, the scientists, the physicists, and the medical doctors of his day. It confirms everything – these men know so much more than he does. How can the gods be so wrong?

However, he does notice something these men have in common. These men know so much but they don't seem to know what they do not know. A light goes off in his head. Could that be what the gods meant? That a man who knows what he doesn't know is wiser than a man who knows much but lacks the knowledge of what he doesn't know.

In Asia, Confucius had the same insight, "Real knowledge is to know one's ignorance."

Wisdom is not the absence of ignorance. We are born in ignorance and die in ignorance. Wisdom is about our relationship to this ignorance.

Wisdom to these early Greeks involved having a healthy relationship with ignorance. The unwise have an unhealthy relationship with ignorance. What does having a healthy relationship with ignorance look like? What does an unhealthy relationship with ignorance look like?

These early philosophers were also psychologists. In general, they thought that the greatest and deepest wisdom one can achieve has to do with self-awareness.

Abraham Lincoln is a good example of this self-awareness. He writes about how his mind works in relationship to knowledge and ignorance. Most historians think of Lincoln as having the most superior intellect of any president, "I am slow to learn, as slow to forget what I stored. My mind is like a piece of steel, very hard to scratch anything on it and once you get it there almost impossible to rub out. "

Abraham Lincoln in knowing his ignorance and how to work with it accomplished something historians believe was beyond what any other President would have been able to do. He found a way to bring unity to an impossible polarized America.

On the other hand, a recent American president who presented himself as one of the smartest persons alive, had no idea of his vast ignorance. As a result, he polarized America to the brink of destroying our Democracy, bringing a large percentage of society to the depths of stupidity which they may or may not ever dig themselves out of. This ignorance was well known by friend and foe, by those working close to him and those who listened to him in the public square, but this ignorance was not known by this president.

To these early Greeks the rich life was a wise life. "Know Thyself" and

"The Unexamined Life is not worth living" was a key that opened that richness. It means knowing your inner truth, your real motives and yes, knowing your ignorance.

A healthy and functional relationship to ignorance awakens the dynamic mind to learning. An unhealthy and dysfunctional relationship to ignorance leads to a static mind and stupidity. You can fix ignorance, but you can't fix stupidity.

The Oxford English dictionary defines ignorance as "lacking knowledge or awareness in general." Note that ignorance is not only lacking knowledge but also awareness. So, to be aware of ignorance, to have knowledge about ignorance, is not ignorant.

I will use the word "stupidity" to describe the opposite when both knowledge and awareness about ignorance are absent.

There are three dominant instinctual impulses we all experience that play an important role in whether we have a healthy or unhealthy relationship to our ignorance: Desire – Fear – Belief. This has more to do with our psychological life than our IQ.

CHAPTER TWO

WHEN DESIRE SHAPES OUR REASONING VERSUS WHEN REASONING SHAPES OUR DESIRES

"Sometimes a great deal of intelligence goes into ignorance when the need for illusion is great." (Saul Bellows)

HOME COURT, BEHIND by one point, three seconds to go, fans going wild, the Lakers are ready to inbound the ball under their own basket. Everybody knows the ball is going to Kobe Bryant. Sure enough, Kobe gets open. One bounce of the ball and a quick fake, Kobe goes up for a jump shot and nails it. The referee indicates Kobe got the shot off in time. The stadium erupted, along with my son and me. The Lakers won by one point. What a game!

However, the officials gathered for a re-play to make sure the ball left Koby's hand before the time ran out. The crowd grew quiet as the slow motion video replay appeared on a large screen. Then the groan of the crowd. It became obvious that Kobe still had the tip of his index finger on the ball when the backboard lit up, ending the game. We waited long enough for the refs to confirm. The Lakers lost.

My young son, almost in tears, protested that Kobe really got the shot off in time and that the refs were a bunch of bums, robbing the Lakers of their win. He was not alone. As we walked out of the stadium, large groups of fans made the same protest. We all saw the same video. It was very clear. Where did this violation of reality come from? How did this ignorance grow as more and more fans joined the protest?

If we want to understand the workings of our own mind as well as the minds of others, we will need to understand the role that desire plays in relationship to reason and reality. A moment of activated passion can overwhelm that moment of reality and create an illusion. The fans got their win, then it was taken away. What can you expect?

From the beginning of time this issue was self-evident and foremost in the minds of humans trying to understand these opposing tensions they were experiencing. In Homer, eight centuries before Christianity, the gods Apollo and Dionysus represent this dynamic (remember the gods don't create humans in their image, we create gods in our image).

Apollo is the god of reason, calm, structured, orderly, thoughtful while Dionysus is the god of passion, uninhibited, instinctual, wild, unrestrained. They are brought together and integrated in the Greek tragedies of Aeschylus and Sophocles four centuries later.

When Christianity arrived, these opposing tensions were dealt with differently. These biological desires were dangerous. They have no value. They are evil. They were thought to have no place in human life. They cannot be integrated. They must be extinguished and defeated.

"For the longings of the flesh are contrary to the Spirit, and those of the spirit are contrary to the flesh; they are in opposition to each other...those who belong to Christ have crucified the flesh with its passions and desires." (Galatians 5).

This theme is with almost equal accuracy, be it called a Hindu or Buddhist or Muslim. One great theme of the great religions is demonic temptations. In the Bible and Koran there is Satan. In Buddhist scripture it is Mara.

———◦✕◦———

Of course, crucifying a major part of one's brain didn't turn out so well. First, it didn't work. Nature always wins out in the end and secondly, we now know the psychological damage inflicted by such an endeavor. Destroying any natural part of ourselves weakens the whole. We can never be whole with such an attitude. We will never be fully alive. We will never feel the confidence and personal power of a true self, a thinking self, a creative, responsible, independent self, connected to reality.

A delusion is believing in something that is not true, something that can be proven false. An illusion is believing in something that we wish were true. It may be true, or it might not be. What is characteristic of illusions is that they are derived from human wishes. These wishes have the force to alter reality.

My son along with many Laker fans were caught in an illusion: what they desired to be true had a greater force than what appeared on the big screen.

If we didn't know before, we certainly know now that Donald Trump had no respect for truth, only delusions and illusions. It started with his presidential campaign convincing his followers that President Obama was not born in America, but in Africa, not one of us. Obama's birth in Hawaii was an absolute fact, but it created an illusion for many.

He ended his presidency the same way, claiming he really won the 2020 election by a land slide and that the election results were nothing but a massive fraud. No election results were more researched than the 2020 results. Each fraud claim was explored by the courts and trained examiners, finding no fraud. Trump lost the election; it was factual from the beginning and constantly confirmed by continuous research.

The January 6th committee put the final nail in Trump's illusion for all to see. Many government officials who supported Trump and wanted the election to be fraudulent testified Trump's claimed were nothing but an illusion when the facts were laid out.

But today as I write this, Trump is wanting to suspend the constitution and reinstate himself as President, because the election was nothing but a massive fraud. Now he appears to be a delusional maniac to truth seekers, but there are still senators and house representatives who support his claims born of his desires, and of course theirs. Trump's desire is for money and power. That desire is at the addictive level and determines his reality. He pursues it with an amazing intensity. He cannot give up. He cannot lose. He can't just go away.

This attack on truth put Americans within a hair of losing their hard fought democracy. How did it come to this? Didn't the people of America see the red flags of stupidity from the beginning? Why didn't this mess become obvious from the beginning? Trump was not clandestine but out there from the beginning. Did not truth matter anymore, or could we not recognize it anymore when challenged? How could we be so ambushed by such an attack on truth that was not even clever or sophisticated? The more outrageous the illusions became, the more they were believed. How did stupidity become so dominant in an educated society? How did the waters of truth get so muddied that society could no longer tell what was true anymore?

Isiah Berlin tells the account of Heidegger and fellow German philosophers watching a parade where Hitler went by, and Heidegger tipped his hat. His colleagues who refused to display antisemitic posters, took him to task for the gesture and Heidegger said, "What's in a tip of a hat?"

On January 30th, 1933, Hitler was sworn in as Chancellor of Germany. On April 21 of the same year Heidegger was elected rector of the University of Freiburg, and his colleagues lost their positions. It was not just Germans, but many Americans gave Hitler a "tip of the hat" before it became too late.

Trump was no Hitler. He had the advantage of being underestimated. He was treated as a harmless buffoon. Every outrageous indiscretion, that would undo any other candidate for the Presidency, was not taken seriously – even when he was caught on tape bragging about how he could get away with "grabbing a woman's pussy" whenever he wanted.

Though a large percentage of the population did not know what they did not know and were unaware of the ignorance before their eyes, there were powerful voices that saw the signs of ignorance rather clearly and were disturbed.

A group of our nation's most respected Mental Health Professionals met at a Yale conference and decided they had an obligation to warn the public of what they saw. This was highly unusual because we psychologists vow to never diagnose a person we are not treating. These psychologists felt that Donald Trump was so out there with his dysfunctions that his diagnosis was not only obvious, but psychologists also are ethically bound to warn people of a dangerous situation.

They wrote a book, THE DANFEROUS CASE OF DONALD TRUMP. If you read those essays today, you realize that the train wreck they saw developing has arrived. They were not unaware of the destructive stupidity others did not see. They predicted the disaster but could not prevent it.

The same awareness was obvious to the Yale historian, Timothy Snyder. He saw the signs of authoritarianism developing and wrote a very readable book for the common person, ON TRYANNY. The attack on truth, finding an enemy, polarizing the people, the destructive cha-risma of developing a mindless fan base – the historical formula for dictatorship that had brought down democracies were on the horizon for Snyder, and he sent out the warning signals and twenty lessons to ward it off for Americans.

One of the world's most distinguished diplomats and political sci-entist, Madeleine Albright, weighed in on this warning. In her book FACISM: A WARNING, Albright who experienced as a child the hor-rors in war-torn Europe between Democracy and Fascism (authoritari-anism) was certain that the world would strongly reject any spiritual successors of Hitler and Mussolini should they arrive in our era. Now she was questioning this assumption.

She states that the momentum toward Democracy that swept the world when the Berlin Wall fell has gone in reverse in many European countries. But her main concern she says is that the United States, which championed the free world, is led by a president who exacer-bates divisions and heaps scorn on democratic institutions.

The warnings continued to come from experienced, mature, and ac-complished thinkers from many disciplines who were not politically driven.

We will revisit this in more detail later. There was more to this than just illusion. Lying about the truth is different than an illusion.

The German philosopher Schopenhauer writes, "We do not want something because we have found reason to have it; we find reasons to have the things we want."

The instinctual brain is more powerful than the thinking brain. The instinctual brain seeks pleasure and avoids pain. The instinctual brain does not think, it reacts. That is not necessarily a bad thing. If we are taking a walk and see a shadow heading toward our head, we auto-matically duck. Only later do we become aware of whether ducking was necessary or not. If we didn't react and instead waited to find out if it was necessary to duck or not, we'd be dead.

The instinctual brain is concerned with survival. It's wired to avoid danger and pain. It's primary. The thinking brain is concerned with learning. It's secondary. Stupidity takes place when we use our instinctual brain when our thinking brain is needed and use our thinking brain when our instinctual brain is needed.

Passion without reason is disastrous, passion with reason is powerful. Impulses, urges, sensations, instant gratifications, recklessly seeking pleasure, caught in the orgiastic force without restraint, mindlessly satisfying hungers are just a part of the way the instinctual brain does business. Greed is a product of malevolent desire. It often leads to arrogance and cruelty. Malevolent desires also create ambitions that make men bullies and deceitful.

When your teenage daughter falls in love with a "bad boy" does reasoning with her have any affect? When a drug addict craves his fix does his reasoning brain have a chance?

What about everyday conflicts? We have a chance to steal something we really want but can't afford, knowing we'll never be caught. We have a chance to satisfy sexual hunger without our partner ever knowing. We gain an advantage if we use deceit. We present ourselves with virtuous motives, when deep down we know it is self-serving and manipulative.

It's human nature to find our urges more powerful than our ethics and we all live with regrets and secrets. Our thinking brain can acknowledge guilt and gain wisdom from our indiscretions; our instinctual brain will repress, deny, or rationalize them away, keeping us stupid.

> "I pass a window in the night,
> A half-dressed lady comes in sight.
> I tell my eyes to look away,
> But they don't hear a word I say." (The author)

On the other hand, the instinctual brain, in the service of learning, can be a powerful force. We often learn more from painful experiences than pleasurable ones. We forget many pleasurable experiences; painful ones seem to stay with us forever. A childhood friend has provided years of positive experiences, but the one I remember most is the one betrayal that ended the friendship.

Divorces end badly. The whole marriage gets blasted, from beginning to end, even though the marriage had its share of happiness and pleasure at one time.

Mark Twain said, "The cat who jumped on a hot stove never jumped on a hot stove again, nor a cold one."

Our instinctual brain is active at birth; our thinking brain is not well developed until we are in our late twenties. That's why children need parents and teachers, protecting kids from themselves.

When thinking shapes our desires, we get to enjoy our desires and find them constructive, even intelligent. This integration of our instinctual brain and our thinking brain has been addressed in many ways by different disciplines.

The poet, Kahlil Gibran, writes, "Your soul is oftentimes a battlefield, upon which your reason and your judgement wage war against your passion and your appetite. Your reason and your passion are the rudder and the sails of your seafaring soul. If either your sails or your rudder be broken, you can but toss and drift, or else be held at a standstill in mid-seas. For reason, ruling alone, is a force confining; and passion, unattended, is a flame that burns to its own destruction."

In psychology Freud described this dynamic by referring to the instinctual part of the brain as an "IT" and the reasoning part of the brain as an "I".

"IT" just happened. "IT" just came to me. The Devil made me do "IT". "IT" wasn't me; something came over me. I just thought of "IT". Being automatically reactive, the "IT" doesn't always feel like a part of our own brain, but something outside of us.

The philosopher/psychologist Nietzsche said, "A thought comes when 'IT' wants, not when 'I' want."

Freud used an analogy of a wild horse and the skilled rider. The wild horse being the "IT" with unrestrained energy and the skilled rider, the "I", directing and managing that energy. In a chariot race a wild horse will crash and burn, but if that energy can be harnessed and channeled that horse will outrace a tame horse. But the driver has no easy task. That powerful horse does not always want to go where the driver wants it to go. This is a common conflict between the "I" and the "IT" and the driver only has intelligence on his side while the horse has all the power.

The "IT" is a cauldron full of seething excitations. The "IT" is filled with energy, has no organization, produces no collective will, only striving to satisfy the intense wants in front of him. The logical laws of thought do not apply to the "IT" and the contrary impulses exist side by side, without cancelling each other out or diminishing each other.

The "IT" does not correspond to space and time and has no recognition of time. "IT" knows no judgement or morality and only seeks discharge at the rawest level.

Unfortunately, Freud's terms got Latinized in translation. The "IT" became the "ID" and the "I" became the "EGO", losing their linguistical punch. Freud thought a healthy psychological life was when both the "IT" and the "I" are strong and active, but always the "I" in control.

The English philosopher John Stuart Mill puts it this way, "Desires and impulses are as much a part of a perfect human being, as beliefs and restraints: and strong impulses are only perilous when not properly balanced. It is not because men's desires are strong that they act ill; it is because their consciences are weak. Strong impulses are another name for energy. The danger which threatens human nature is not the excess, but the deficiency, of personal impulses."

The instinct that goes into a murderous rage is the same instinct that rushes into a burning building to save lives.

Instincts have their own wonderful form of intelligence. This intelligence comes quickly without thinking. Good athletes have good instincts. When a baseball player comes to the plate, he has to face a baseball coming at him, in the range of 100 miles an hour. The ball can dip at the last moment or can curve in either direction depending on the spin of the ball. It can be slower or faster than it looks. The thinking mind will not do. The batter's instinctual mind has to read the spin on the ball, how fast the ball is coming, whether it's dangerously coming at his head or how close to being a strike, something to swing at – all in split second. Only a developed instinct can do that successfully.

There are many situations we all face in life when we have to depend on our instincts. We just know something is not right even though we can't prove it. Our intuition alerts us to both dangers and opportunities. This knowledge comes to us all at once. The philosopher Pascal acknowledged, "The heart has its reason that reason knows nothing of."

We get in trouble when we use our fast thinking, when slow thinking is required and use our slow thinking when fast thinking is required; when we use our instinctual thinking when our logical thinking is required and use our logical thinking when instinctual thinking is required.

Prisons are filled with men whose violence is triggered in a heartbeat over nothing. Many of them never find self-regulation over their triggers and remain dangerous to themselves and others.

On the other hand, making love is most pleasurable when we let go and let our instincts take over and tragically boring when the sexual manual and guidelines takes over. When arguments get heated, we get stupid when we become reactive and lose our slow thinking thoughtful mind.

We begin to gain wisdom when we come to terms with the fact that there is a great gulf between our wishes and reality. Stupidity is expecting that reality should coincide with our wishes. We wish we were taller or thinner or stronger or better looking or smarter or richer or younger and the list goes on. We wish our children were more brilliant and outstanding than the children around them. Stupidity is wishing for the life we want, instead of investing in the life available to us.

Another characteristic of instinctual wishes is the fact that they easily become insatiable. Not only is it impossible for the realities of life to satisfy the wishes, but even when the wish is satisfied, it's never enough. It always wants more.

The essence of reason shaping pleasure is knowing that pleasure tends to dissipate and leave the mind agitated, hungry for more. The idea that just more dollar, one more rung on the ladder will lead to satisfying this desire reflects a misunderstanding about human nature. Pleasure shaping reason is built into human nature; we are designed to feel the next goal will bring bliss, but the bliss is designed to evaporate shortly after we get there.

The idea that injecting heroin is fun keeps infecting people by appealing to the pleasure seeking brain, rarely to the ultimate advantage of those people.

How long does it take before the partner of your dreams becomes disappointing and you want more from him or her? How long does it take before your possessions become less satisfying because you notice those who have more than you?

The truth that pleasure is ephemeral; that its constant pursuit is not a reliable source of happiness is not easily grasp. Our pleasure seeking brain is not built for this reality.

"Beware of luxury" is not only captured by the happy minimalist, but by the person who wants to feed and grow the elevated mind.

Growing, developing, creating, living with energy, loving, learning creates more happiness than pure luxury. Most of us have experienced a confusing disconnect when we hear about a person who has all the riches, fame, and luxuries of life, committing suicide.

Do the same religions that fear biological pleasures, on the other hand feed pleasurable illusions. "The grass is greener on the other side the fence" is the illusion created by desire.

Is not the grass greener on the other side of death also? "He's now in a better place. She is now free of her pain. He is united with his loved ones waiting for him. She is in a place where there are no more tears, no more heartaches, no painful separations. He is at peace at last. She is experiencing a kind of joy unknown to this world," is the common rhetoric at funerals.

Is this rhetoric born out of solid, well proven evidence or out of something we wish were true? Is this the role of religion, to keep us from suffering the painful realities of our mortality? If this is an illusion so what? What harm does it do for an illusion to help get a person through a dark night? Or once we court stupidity in any area of our lives do we compromise our thinking mind? Does compromising the integrity of any part of our mind affect the whole? Does courting illusions dilute the learning process of a rigorous mind?

On the other hand, the agnostic mind that wishes these things to be true is not stupid. His agnosticism saves him and allows him to enjoy his dreams and imaginations.

Science seems to be the one intelligence that takes us into objective reality, outside ourselves, into the world of nature, into the infinity of the cosmos. It takes its own course whether we like it or not, whether we approve of it or not. The tornado never swerves off course to miss a hospital or a school yard. An iceberg never discerns whether it's a friendly ship or an enemy ship.

We understand a mother believing her son was framed in a crime when the proof is beyond the shadow of doubt. We understand why a child's sport hero is better than his or her friend's sport hero. We understand why denials, rationalizations and other defense mechanisms take hold inside us when we face unpleasant realities. We understand why prejudice is something we all deal with. We can understand that when this life brings unjust humiliations, we desire that justice will be dished out in the next. We both fear and desire Karma. The next life is always a life of utopia, the utopia we were robbed of in this life.

A person who is entrenched in a truth born of desire will never be able to have a thoughtful exchange of the matter and will be blind to his or her real motives. If we dislike someone, our desiring brain will dislike everything about the person, even when he or she speaks the truth, or does something virtuous. Desire can be a great source of unhappiness, but it need not be. Under wise management, desire can become a great source of pleasure and happiness.

The Epicureans made pleasure and desire their highest value and interest, but they were far from "hedonistic." We can learn a lot from these early Greeks. They believed that "happiness was the absence of pain." The movement from all the forms of discomfort to comfort was the source of greatest pleasure. The pleasure of a cold drink of water is greatest when you are hot and thirsty. The real pleasures of life were modest, prudent, and simple. There is no greater rest than after a hard day's work. What joy we feel when our nagging tooth ache suddenly goes away. The most enjoyable meal comes when we are extremely hungry.

Going from discomfort to comfort is constant and often unconscious. We move in our chair and in bed to get more comfortable automatically. We find pleasure in comfortable social situations, in the food that tastes good, and the activities that are fun. We are wired to avoid pain and seek pleasure.

Think of the guy who wakes up on a Sunday morning, grumpy and bored though he has a free day to do what he wants. Nothing interests him. He goes to McDonalds for coffee and stops at the grocery store for a few items in a rather robotic space. Back home his wife asks, "What's wrong" and he says, "Nothing."

Suddenly he realizes his wallet is gone. Frantically he begins his search with no luck. Now he begins to panic. Driver's license, credit cards, a list of passwords, a couple hundred dollars and loads of other information he can't bear to lose. He alerts his wife and they both try to figure out where his wallet might be. In distress he traces his way back to McDonalds, back to the grocery store, still nothing. Finally, he gives up, prepares himself for what's ahead of him. His day is ruined. In that moment he feels like his life will be ruined for the next couple weeks.

Then his wife shouts out from the other room, "I found it!"

He rushes to her and in sheer delight sees his wallet in her hands. He hugs her and says they should celebrate and do something special today. With wallet in hand, he is suddenly the happiest man alive.

What happened? Nothing really changed in his life outwardly than when he woke up in a bad mood. He had his wallet then.

What happened was that he experienced a deep distress and discomfort in losing his wallet and in finding it, the distress went away and left him in a state of happiness. Very Epicurean.

Something to be said for the old silly joke of the guy hitting his head against the wall. When asked why he was doing it he answered, "Because it feels so good when I stop."

Desire provides aliveness, a meaning, an energy, a pleasure that no person in his or her right mind would want to live without. Life would become unbearable. A life without desire is not a life worth living. Structuring desire is the key. The French are known for getting the most out of desire as a hunger, as an appetite.

A night with friends at a French Cafe will start out with a drink. They take their time. After a while they share some appetizers, both satisfying the hunger and keeping it alive. Later the main meal arrives. It is not gobbled down, but meticulously savoring every bite. More conversation before the dessert arrives and sometime later after dinner drinks. Only then do the scrapes of food that once provoked and sustained pleasure, turn into garbage. The desire is gone once it is totally satisfied, also the pleasure until the next time. However, they made that pleasure last for hours. They tried to get the most of it before it disappeared. Again, very Epicurean.

In Milan Kundera's novel, SLOWNESS, he refers to the 18th century narrative where the marvelous Madame de T summons a young nobleman to her chateau one evening and gives him an unforgettable lesson on the pleasures of making love. There are three stages to this romantic and erotic evening. In the first stage they take a long walk in the park. The nobleman has to manage his arousal during their long, but interesting conversations. This opens the door to the second stage.

They find their way into the Pavilion and begin to make love. The foreplay is not rushed, no delirium or mad love racing toward orgasms. She is a master of the art of staying in the state of arousal. Then she cuts it off and they go back to the park. They sit on a bench. She points out the rooftops, the trees and everything to see as darkness takes over and the park and the houses around it light up. Only then does she usher in the third phase.

Now they go into the chateau, and they make love, lengthily and slowly until the break of dawn. Again, very Epicurean.

Our unbridled instincts don't know that taking our time making love to someone whose company we enjoy gives us a pleasure that a drug induced orgy promises but can never produce. The Epicureans knew that the unrealistic search for the hedonistic idea is incompatible to human nature and that the wild search for happiness only leads to more unhappiness robbing us of the simple pleasures available to us when we are free of pain.

There is a big difference between the animal in us rushing toward the satisfaction, the orgasmic, not getting there fast enough, always wanting more, and the human in us who nurtures and values the joy of desiring. For real pleasure, our impulses and urges need to integrate with the slow thinking brain. In that integration the two blend together, moving in and out with each other, losing their sharp distinctions like branches waving wildly in the wind without breaking. This cannot happen if desires shape thinking; only when thinking structures desires. A person who wants to pursue wisdom and avoid stupidity will always be willing to introspect his or her real motives – whether they are born of desire or reality.

It is difficult for our civilized and moral minded self to face our most primitive impulses that can and will get triggered at times. A patient says, "I can't imagine someone wishing another person dead."

I think to myself, "I can't imagine a person who doesn't have moments when he or she wishes someone dead."

Repressing our dark desires only keeps them alive at an unconscious level, reinforcing stupidity. Ghosts that are silenced only get bigger. Facing them reinforces the power of our developing self to take control. Knowing our ignorance makes us wise. Knowing our dark side makes us wise and virtuous.

The English philosopher, Bertrand Russel, said that politicians often present something as virtuous when the real motive is a quest for power.

The Danish philosopher, Soren Kierkegaard, said, "We can only understand life backwards, but must live it forward." Sometimes our wishful thinking proves to be true when time allows us to play it backwards, and sometimes not. Active thinking is not omnipotent. Wishful thinking allows us to take calculated risks that sometimes make good things happen in our lives; things we would have missed out on, had we not acted on it. Following our desires get us an education, work we enjoy and financial stability. It can push us to achieve things we thought impossible but find out differently.

Peter Bergen's book, THE RISE AND FALLL OF OSAMA BIN LADEN, talks about the negotiations the United States had with the Taliban leaders in leaving Afghanistan. They believed (and hoped) that the Taliban were no longer a terrorist group but could govern and negoti- ate with other nations. But when the United States left, the Taliban leadership became a safe haven for old guard terrorists, including Ayman al- Zawahri. Bergen says that it turned out to be "wishful thinking" on the part of the United States. But that could have gone either way. Only playing it backwards did the United States come to know the truth. It doesn't necessarily mean it was unwise to give it a chance to be different.

It doesn't mean that wishful thinking cannot have value in our lives. Being right all the time is not meant for humans. Does any intelligent being think fortune tellers can give us knowledge of the future? Yet they make a living. The important thing is to recognize wishful think- ing for what it is and what it is not.

We have the saying, "Fool me once, shame on you; fool me twice, shame on me."

The desiring brain and the thinking brain are not always in conflict. Intelligence allows us to go after the things we want in life. Intelligence gives us a better chance to make our desires reality. Intelligence, then, is the ability to attain goals in the face of obstacles by means of decisions based on rational (truth-obeying) rules. Experiencing the difference between reasoning shaped desires and desired shaped rea- soning on a personal level helps us recognize this dynamic socially and politically.

Knowing how desire shapes our reality can help us avoid the unreal- istic expectations we put on ourselves and others. Our unmet, unre- alistic desires make us judgmental and disappointed in relationships that are "good enough."

The English psychoanalyst and pediatrician Winnicott, introduces us to the term "good enough." We only need to be a "good enough" parent to facilitate good child development. No heroic parenting is needed.

What does an acorn need to become an oak tree? It only needs a good enough environment. It can handle some bad winds and periods of drought or too much rain. It only needs things to be good enough and not too bad. The same is for "good enough" partners, friends, and work that can provide a happy life and satisfying relationships. Unrealistic desires create more pain than pleasure. To embrace our humanity is to be realistic. One of life's tragedies is to realize how important someone or something was in our life only when it's gone.

In my early life as a pastor, I conducted many a funeral when I really wanted to say:

> "I'm the one who failed you so,
> those many times you told me so.
> Your words were harsh,
> your heart grew cold,
> didn't get much better,
> as we grew old.
> Today you cried you loved me so,
> so hard to just survive.
> It would have meant so much to me,
> to hear those words when still alive."
>
> In THE PROPHET, Kahlil Gibran says, "Love knows not its own depth until the hour of separation."
> Who among us has not experienced that reality?

THREE

WHEN FEAR SHAPES OUR REASONING VERSUS WHEN REASONING SHAPES OUR FEAR

"We fear things we need not fear and don't fear the things we should fear." (Sigmund Freud's definition of what he called the "neurotic" part of our brain)

IF DESIRES, FREE of self-regulation, can take over our rational mind, instinctual fear is ever as powerful to do the same.

Riding my dirt bike on a trail in the San Bernadino mountains, I see a rattlesnake curled up on the trail a few feet ahead. My instinctual brain shoots me full of adrenalin (instincts use adrenalin that makes us stronger and quicker to avoid danger). I lift up my legs and shout out to my friend behind me, "Rattle Snake," as I run over the creature as it leaps up to get me. My friend also runs over the creature with the same adrenalin rush.

We park our bikes. We get a long branch and carefully go back to where the snake was. It's still there all curled up. Did we kill it riding over it? Staying a good distance away, the adrenalin still in our veins I poke at the snake with my long branch. My friend looks at me in amazement and can't stop laughing. There was no snake, just a curled up stick with knots on the ends; knots that sprang up when we rode over the stick.

Our instinctual brain (the amygdala) did its job. The stick was a close enough resemblance to a snake for our instinctual brain to send out a danger signal, and we reacted likewise. The instinctual brain will always error on side of safety. Only when we used our slow thinking brain to check out the situation, did we learn there was nothing to fear.

A threat perceived sets off an automatic body alarm and creates a physiological response, whether it's a battlefield, an oncoming car, or a stick that looks like a snake.

One of the most revered names in football is NFL Coach and TV commentator, John Madden. In 1960, sixteen football players, a student manager and a football booster from Cal Poly died in a plane crash. Madden was not on the plane, but he lost a lot of people who were close to him. In 1979 he had a panic attack on a flight and never flew again. Here is a man who had to travel constantly, often coast to coast. From then on, he did it only by bus.

Because he was famous and well loved, Greyhound Lines supplied a custom bus with driver without cost to him. Madden and his bus trips became a part of Madden's legend.

The irrational paradox of Madden's situation was this: what made him feel safe, traveling the country in a bus, statistically put him in greater danger than taking a plane. His bus trips meant traveling all night on all kinds of roads and weather.

Madden, being highly educated and one of football's best minds, was completely aware of this irrationality, but no matter how hard he tried, his rational thinking could never free him of his phobia. Even though he was self-aware of this ignorance, the frontal cortex (the reasoning brain) could never get the higher hand. The imagined threat from the amygdala always got triggered leaving him helpless to fly.

His self-awareness saved him from a state of stupidity. He was well aware of the irrationality. He knew his ignorance, even though he could never completely control It. But this insight, this awareness, did not rob him of a certain wisdom in this matter.

Most of us are aware of the many phobias there are and how both the rich and famous, along with the common person, are affected by them.

There are times in human life when irrational stimuli are too powerful for our rational thinking, but what spares us from being stupid about it is our awareness of this ignorance. If we refer to it as paranoia or a mental dysfunction, we are not ignorant; we just know we need to get help, so it doesn't limit our lives in a negative way. When we fail to discern between a rational fear and an irrational fear, that's when we're in trouble. That's when fear shapes our reality, and we lose our good mind.

One can be easily controlled through fear. People who strive for power and control over others find fear not only effective, but essential. Psychologists have discovered that we are hard wired for bad news overpowering good news. That's why fear is an effective means of gaining control.

If you want blind obedience from a child, make him fear you. Fear, shame, and punishment are your best tools. Of course, you will damage his psyche, sometimes beyond repair, but you will get an obedient child.

In THE PRINCE Nicolo Machiavelli addresses a monarch's difficulty in retaining authority telling him, "It is better to be feared than loved."

Angela Merkel has a fear of dogs, of which Vladimir Putin is very aware. They met together in Moscow in January 2007 over energy issues. At some point Putin let his two large dogs into the room.

Even in Democratic elections, candidates will always appeal to fear in order get elected, some more than others; fear of all the things one should worry about if the other candidate gets elected. Some will go so far as to paint a picture of the utter disaster of the present situation and present themselves as a messianic figure who can save the world on the verge of destruction.

In THE FLAG AND THE CROSS: WHITE CHRISTIAN NATIONALISM AND THE THREAT TO AMERICAN DEMOCRACY, Gorski and Perry research how Donald Trump, a non-religious person, captured the support of white Christian nationalism. White Christian nationalists believe American was ordained by God to be a Christian nation, the new promised land. The success of the United States is part of God's plan, and the Federal Government should advocate Christian values. Indigenous groups and minorities stand in the way. The legacy of slavery is a danger to the country's authentic identity.

Gorski and Perry were shocked by the unexpected response to their research on what was the greatest threat to this group. They saw the greatest threat as coming not from Atheists or Muslims, but from "socialists."

Trump understood the dog-whistle power of "socialism" and appealed to this fear. He warned that "the extreme left in America is trying to replace religion with government and replace God with socialism." He promised the crowd that "America will never be a socialist country because America was not built by religious-hating socialists."

The union of politics and religion was complete. That was the group who believed they were the most persecuted group in America. That appeal to their fears by Trump wedded them to Trump no matter what, and later stormed the capital with Christian nationalist symbols.

Timothy Snyder, the Yale historian, warns us of this blueprint in his book, ON TYRANNY. Tyranny often overwhelms democracies because fear is a powerful and active instinctual force. When in trouble our immature minds turn to the strong father, both on earth and "our Father who art in heaven." As it is said, "there are no atheists in foxholes." In ancient cultures great leaders were turned into gods. In a personality cult, the authoritarian leader is treated as a god. Democracies are prey to authoritarian leaders because of the fear factor. Contemporary American politics are facing that crisis too.

Recently the FBI got a search warrant to retrieve important documents that were stored at Trump's residence, that needed to be safely stored back in Washington. After many attempts to get Trump to co-operate, this became the last resort. They went to his residence and retrieved the documents safely. They did not arrive in a threatening way. No weapons were drawn, no one had to worry about being arrested, no one would be harmed, they were only after the boxes that needed to be stored in Washington. Mission accomplished without harm to anyone.

Days later Sean Hannity appeared on the news and said something like this if not verbatim, "The FBI just raided the personal residence of Donald Trump. Once they get away with that watch out. Trump supporters better be careful how you 'dot' your 'I's' or cross your "T's" because next they'll be coming after you."

I laughed out loud and said to my wife, "What an idiot." That was as good an example as you could give of a logical fallacy one would learn on Philosophy 101, if not before. It's called "a false equivalency."

Certainly, one would not have to know it had a name in order to see the irrationality – that a peaceful retrieving of documents that had to find their way back to Washington, after all other attempts failed is equivalent to raiding your home and arresting you because you might have voted for Trump. How could anyone not see the irrationality? How could anyone not see the motive was to denigrate the FBI and provoke an irrational fear?

My wife did not laugh. She shuddered, "That stuff works today."

In playing with other children a child often finds the parent in the way, but when the child becomes afraid the child can't get to the parent fast enough.

Every parent knows how much time is spent teaching a child to both overcome fears and to know what to fear. I remember standing in a shallow pool urging my little girl to jump into my outstretched arms. I still see her standing there crouched over, both wanting to jump and fearing to do so. I'm in the pool assuring her it is safe, and her mother is in a lounge chair cheering her on. Finally, I go to her, take her in my arms and walk around the pool getting her used to the water. Later we try again, and she jumps. Now she wants to do it all the time. She feels safe even though she feels a rush each time I take a few steps backward. Soon I have to be careful because she'll jump when I'm not looking. Mind you, this is the same child that wants to let go of my hand when crossing a street.

The instinctual fear of strangers has been largely studied by sociologists. It's as old as Sapiens. We see it in newborns. As the baby grows the infant is comforted by familiar faces and troubled when a strange face appears, much like most animals.

A playful and friendly dog can turn vicious when a stranger appears. Racism and immigration are prey to this dynamic.

We accept that children are fully driven by instinct and weak in intelligence. But adults cannot remain children forever. Even if our instinctual life is much more powerful than our educational life, reality mostly wins out in the end. We humans are creatures of weak intelligence, ruled by instinctual desires and fears in need of an education in reality. It's nice to know that.

Irrational fear comes in many forms: Phobia's - an exaggerated and illogical fear; Paranoias - irrational suspiciousness, and distrustfulness of others; Obsessions - uncontrolled thoughts of everything that could go wrong and turn dangerous; Anxiety attacks - that seem to come out of nowhere, are all popular on that list.

Many psychologists believe that phobias are innate fears that have never been unlearned.

Now remember, experiencing any of these irrational fears does not make us stupid, it is only when we are not aware that these irrational fears are ignorant that we become stupid. Knowing one's ignorance is what makes us wise. Being aware of these ignorance's and understanding these ignorance's give us a better chance to overcome them, but even if we can't, at least we are not ignorant of their ignorance.

Self-awareness, the ability to think consciously about ourselves is uniquely human and clearly distinguishes us from animals. All animals think, but no animal can think consciously about itself in the complex and abstract ways that we can. Self-awareness allows us to evaluate ourselves and gives us a chance to purposefully change.

Evolutionary Psychology also chips in with some interesting ideas that help explain this problem, natural to us all. We once thought that the first humans were Adam and Eve, created by a Deity about five thousand years ago. Now we know humans have been around for over a million years. Fear is the emotion that motivated our ancestors to the dangers they were likely to face. Our brain, our instincts developed around these fears. These fears still stay with us when they no longer apply to modern situations.

Snakes and spiders have been scary from the beginning of time. Many spiders and snakes were venomous and dangerous for the hunters and gatherers who came upon them constantly. Their fear was not a phobia. Today we ought to be afraid of guns, driving too fast, driving without a seatbelt, lighter fluid, and hair dryers near bathtubs, not of snakes and spiders.

Why with centuries of culture and education are we still such an aggressive people? Our primitive brain may come into play. Biologists largely agree that our human brains have not changed that much in respect to civilization's advances. In modern society, outbursts of deadly aggression are rarely beneficial to anyone. But in the days before we had our current culture and law enforcement, each person had to fend off threats with aggression when necessary. Nonaggressive individuals simply would not have survived at the same rate, and their offspring would have been at risk as well.

The fear of strangers made sense to primitive tribes. But today it's out of stupidity that we fear people who don't look like us, dress like us, or speak our language. Familiarity and security go hand in hand instinctually even today with reason at times. But to the primitive human, it had a greater role.

Today we have greater protection from the elements of nature like storms, freezing and sun-scorching weather. Think of the brain that primitive humans needed for these things.

Today not being loved by someone creates a temporary psychological pain, but when we treat it as if our survival is at stake, we might be tapping into our primitive brain that has not yet caught up with today's reality. Being rejected by your tribe meant death. No one could make it on their own.

Does overeating have a connection to our primitive brain? During virtually all of human evolution, our days were spent looking for food and when we found some, it made sense to eat as much as possible because we had no way to store or carry extra food, and we didn't know when we'd eat again.

Perhaps evolution helps us experience how looking out of a tall building can trigger our fear of heights; totally irrational. But for millions of years, when people looked down from a very high place, they were probably up a tree or at the edge of a cliff. We are descendants of people who felt those fears, not of those who were careless and didn't survive.

Earlier I spoke of religion as an illusion, derived from human wishes. How nice it would be if there was a God who created the world and was a benevolent Providence, and that there were a moral order in the universe and an afterlife. But fear also plays a part. For some, religion is a great comfort, but for many it carries great fears. God punishes us if we don't keep his commandments. God sends unbelievers to an eternal hell. Some become believers out of fear and find little comfort in it.

In the seventeenth century the philosophe Blaise Pascal made a pragmatic argument for the belief In God, called Pascal's Wager. The argument boils down to this: If you believe in God and find out He doesn't exit you have nothing to lose, but if you don't believe in God and you find He exists you have everything to lose; you'll burn in Hell. Pascal's argument for belief in God is not born out of reason but out of fear.

The German philosopher/psychologist Nietzsche said, "Fear is the mother of morality." If we fear something our instinctual brain will make it immoral. Those moralistic rules are opposed to scientific and other forms of intellectual development. They are guided by moral principles that disregard reality-based notions of good and evil. Interracial marriage was once immoral, and slavery was moral.

Trying to save a Jew was immoral in Nazi Germany and Huckleberry Finn should have turned his friend Jim over to authorities in his America.

In THE SCARLET LETTER by Nathanial Hawthorn, the woman accused of adultery must wear a scarlet letter (A for adultery) around her neck because the men of the community feared that if she got away unpunished, then their own wives would think it was okay. There was no such punishment for a man because men who cheated didn't create the same fear because men made the rules.

In 1811 England, a Luddite was a member of a group who destroyed machinery, mainly in the cotton industry because it threatened their jobs. Today we use the term for the person who opposes new technology out of fear. Today we have political luddites. We have members of the republican party who will lose their positions of privilege if they oppose Trump, even though they know Trump is dangerous for our country. They cannot get reelected without his approval and his voters. They cannot do what they know is right and reasonable because they fear the loss of their position which is far from an irrational fear, but a fear that compromises their morality and reality. It's easy to be disgusted at this, while also being sympathetic to their situation. But we also have examples of those who were heroic and suffered for their commitment to truth, reason, and reality, at personal expense.

It is not an easy task for reason to shape fear, when fear is such a powerful force that easily overpowers reason. But humans have resources to do something about that. Understanding irrational fears in ourselves helps us unmask malevolent motives of destructive charisma leaders so popular in our world today. No dictator or authoritarian government can ever rule a people without stirring up their fear. The fearful mind is prey to authoritarianism, often in the form of the strong man.

I have learned much from my conversations with men embracing the gun culture. The perceived threat is that the Government wants to take away their freedom and taking way their guns is the first step.

The only reason I still have my freedom as a non-gun owner is because the Government knows there are well armed men out there. Their guns are protecting me whether I know it or not. I don't need to own a gun to feel safe because they do.

Any attempt to nudge them toward more reasonable thinking only reinforced to them how naive I was.

Their fears keeps them from realizing that freedom in the hands of gun owners, instead of democratic institutions creates the very authoritarianism they are trying to avoid.

CHAPTER **FOUR**

WHEN BELIEF SHAPES REASONING VERSUS WHEN REASONING SHAPES BELIEF

A BELIEF IS an organized and settled state of the mind of what is perceived as real. It is born out of mental chaos and confusion. It is as much, instinctual as desire and fear - for humans to unconsciously organize raw sensations, overwhelming stimuli, and chaotic impulses, into an organized system in order to avoid madness. Beliefs give one confidence in a structure of truth authorized by the traditions of one's culture. We cannot live without beliefs. We are hard wired to develop beliefs. Otherwise, our minds would not survive.

Beliefs become a dogmatic system set in concrete when reason no longer shapes beliefs, but when a belief system determines reason.

Churchill said," Some people change their principles for the sake of their party – others change their party for the sake of their principles."

The Middle Ages are called the Middle Ages because it was the middle time of history between the 4th century and roughly the 15th century. The vibrant Greco-Roman culture gave way to the rise of

Christianity in the 4th century. That period is also called the Dark Ages because the church ruled by dogma, putting to death scientific and cultural achievements. Authoritarianism ruled the Middle Ages. The Renaissance (meaning revival, reviving scientific and cultural achievements) was an intellectual revolution approaching the 15th century which led to the Reformation (a religious revolution) which in turn led to the Enlightenment period of the 17th century. The Enlightenment period is often called, "The Age of Reason."

During this middle time in history, Christian dogma revealed by God became the ruler of all thought. Any thought that questioned this absolute dogma called orthodoxy (correct belief) was considered heretical, punishable by death. Little wonder that the Middle Ages is also known as the Dark Ages and that men like Descartes born in 1596 had to walk a tight rope before culture embraced the idea that the enlightened individual was a better source of wisdom than Church dogma.

Reason, not Dogma, became the zeitgeist of the 17th and 18th century. That general intellectual, moral, and cultural climate became the spirit of the day and energized the philosophers of that time. Today we have a library of their writings. However, their audiences were their fellow philosophers and seldom the public, which makes them difficult to understand.

Descartes, along with his colleagues and followers are often thought to be the fathers of the Enlightenment period. The philosophical thinking that the enlightened individual was a better source of wisdom than church dogma ended the Dark/Middle Ages which the Renaissance and Reformation began.

Christianity itself split over these issues during the Protestant Reformation, mainly led by the rebel priest Martin Luther, who believed every believing individual should be his own priest, known as, "The Priesthood of Believers." These Protestants (protesters) thought that the individual conscience of a believer was a better source of morality than the corrupted doctrines of the Church. The dogma that salvation and favors from God to deceased loved ones could be purchased with money to the Church, was the nail in the coffin of Catholicism for Luther.

In the Dark Ages the Church did not believe in integrating the instinctual brain with the cognitive brain. Born of a Pietist Methodist, German Puritan mother in 1724, Immanuel Kant is often considered the greatest philosopher by philosophers themselves when it comes to his contribution on how the mind works. He believed that the mind developed from chaos to order.

Every human being has a part of the brain that seeks order out of the mind's sensations, basic urges, stimuli, impulses, perceptions, etc. That part of the brain organizes the chaotic mind, like a person who puts the pieces of a jigsaw puzzle together to form a complete picture.

Kant thought of the mind as an inherent structure with a movement that is always toward order, sequence, unity, and integration. When early humans looked at the chaotic multitude of stars, they created constellations to bring a pattern to the heavens. Once they mapped out the heavens, they never saw the chaotic heavens again. Modern humans pick out these same patterns. Once you learn about the constellations you will never see a chaotic sky again, even if you try. We could also say, once we recognize these constellations, we will never see the real sky again. It's just the way our minds are wired.

That part of the brain takes the raw material of our instinctual chaos and organizes it into a mindful whole. It is phylogenetic, a particular feature of the human species that seeks stability out of instability, to regain balance when we've lost our footing, to organize our garage when the mess gets too much, to clean up the house after a party, to find a place for everything laying around, to file important papers that are in a pile cluttering our desk.

The mind is driven likewise, to organize all the unconnected pieces of the mind into an organized whole, a Gestalt (a whole made up of many parts). We develop belief systems, synthesize mental conflicts, always bringing things to completion, having the final say. This completion brings satisfaction, comfort, homeostasis; all things we lose when we are confused and can't find our way out of it.

Imagine the discomfort when we can't finish a jigsaw puzzle because some pieces are missing, maybe only one. We only find this out when we come to the end, but it doesn't feel like the end without all the pieces. We throw away a jigsaw puzzle that is missing pieces. The missing pieces ruin our satisfaction for completion.

This process of going from the unknown to the known, from confusion to making sense, from chaos to order is how the mind grows.

Piaget, the French psychologist who studied cognitive development in children and adults, put it this way: he used three common sense terms to describe this process: assimilation, accommodation, and homeostasis.

When we bring pieces into an organized whole, we feel the stability and comfort, homeostasis. But since knowledge is never absolute or finished, this homeostasis is short lived. We come upon new information that means the whole has to be re-organized. In order to "assimilate" the new information, the whole must "accommodate" it. There goes our "homeostasis" for a while. Only when the whole comes apart in order to come together at a higher level does the homeostasis come back again.

The growing mind cannot make this completion it longs for permanent. It is always a temporary pleasure, like mountain climbers who get to a peak and find the pleasure of accomplishing that climb. But they can only rest for so long until they're off to the next peak.

This drive for completion and permanence is not only the way the mind grows, but it can also become the way the mind destroys itself. It destroys itself when the mind cannot let go of the temporary stability and makes it permanent. The growing mind must always lose its balance, lose its footing for a while in order to grow.

In order for a crab to grow it must shed its shell because the shell of a crab doesn't grow. The crab outgrows its shell and must grow a new shell. When it is between shells it is most vulnerable. The new shell is not in place yet when the old shell is shed.

The growing mind must shed one stage of permanence for another in order to grow and in between permanencies, one must accept uncertainty, confusion, and instability. The organized Gestalt (a whole made up of many parts) must constantly re-organize itself if the mind is to grow. When this whole becomes rigid or saturated, unable to take in new learning, the mind begins to die. Taking on new learning and changing the way one thinks about things as the mind grows brings moments of discomfort.

Think of the trapeze artist swinging from bar to bar. Never letting go of a bar until the artist has a hold of the next leaves the crowd bored, but they gasp with dangerous excitement when they see the artist let go of one bar before the other is there. In that moment the artist is flying through the air between bars and the crowd witnesses their own entertaining fear and clap with relief when the artist grasps the next bar, a rather hyperbolic metaphor of the growing mind.

This discomfort is one of my earliest memories. I was about three years old when I couldn't make sense of the cows and horses in the same pasture. How were they related? It bothered me, until I figured it out, all by myself and I recall the comfort it brought. The cows were mommies, and the horses were daddies. But then one day, sitting on the fence, my older brother spoiled it all by telling me there were mommy cows and daddy cows, mommy horses and daddy horses. In tears I ran into the house, getting my mother to tell my brother how wrong he was. Everything I worked so hard to make sense of came apart.

In chemistry unsaturated elements change when combined with other elements. A saturated element doesn't change when combined with another element. It is a stronger and more stable element, but it can no longer change. The saturated mind feels strong in its certainties, but it no longer grows. It becomes robotic, fixed, machine like.

In the 16th century Copernicus was the first European to assert heliocentrism in his, ON THE REVOLUTION OF THE CELESTIAL SPHERES in 1543 just before his death. This was a threat to church dogma and the church quickly made this theory heretical, in an age where heretics did not fare well.

A few years later, Galileo, an Italian astronomer and physicist, born in 1564, created improved telescopes that allowed him to discover the Galilean moons. He believed in "heliocentrism", that the earth not only spun around each day, but it revolved around the sun, not the other way around. What got Galileo in trouble with the church was that the new information supported the hypothesis. In 1616 he was arrested, put in prison, then house arrest for the rest of his life as a dangerous heretic.

To assimilate and accommodate this new information was too much for the Gestalt of the day. That Gestalt was so threatened that the changes required were impossible. Copernicus' discovery, advanced by Galileo, not only contradicted scripture, but it contradicted the basic dogma that was revealed by God to the Popes. If the scriptures could get things wrong, along with church doctrine, then that whole world would come crashing down. Copernicus was already gone, and his theories were already buried with him. Now Copernicus revisited had to go – Galileo had to go.

Church dogma had found completion in this matter, the religious gestalt had to be preserved. Galileo's life was spared because he recanted his scientific discoveries.

There is a famous painting of Galileo in prison. On the wall scratched in the cement are the words, "And yet it moves."

Belief systems are built on our need for completion. They will always appeal to people who are uncomfortable holding and working with uncertainty and doubt, needing to rush toward uniformed conclusions. Reality always wins out in the end, but in some cases, it might take hundreds of years. Science does not care what we believe, nor is it ever altered by it.

Religion and politics tend to become prey to this. The Gestalt becomes a bubble, a template unmovable. All experiences and discoveries are interpreted within that bubble, the template doesn't change, all phenomena are doctored and spun to enforce the bubble, not alter it. One of the most beloved hymns reflects this longing, "Death and decay, all around I see. O thou who changes not, abide with me."

When I was a boy, it was pretty much accepted by intelligent people that Adam and Eve were real people, the first humans created about six thousand years ago by following biblical genealogies. Today we know that humans appeared about two and a half million years ago. But we can still run into people who believe that the earth was created six thousand years ago.

Darwin not only captured that biological things grow and evolve, but that this has been going on for millions of years. His vision of the depth of time puts him in a class by himself. The discomfort religion suffers from evolutionary science still goes on.

Progressive religions do better with this than conservative ones. Progressive religions have been gradually nudged toward revisions, while conservative religions find it more difficult.

Modern science is often misunderstood because it is committed to research rather than belief. Research discovers new information that reorganizes the present gestalt. The fixed mind rejects science because of this misunderstanding. They say, science once said this… now it says this…how can you trust science? They don't realize that science is not absolute, nor does it try to be. Science can only say that with the information we have today, this is what we believe.

Science loves to prove itself wrong, because that proof advances knowledge, while the fixed mind says, "Don't confuse me with new facts, I've already made up my mind."

The dynamic mind says, "I used to believe that...now I believe this... and five years from now I'm sure I'll go through many more revisions."

When static minds disagree, bitter arguments are exchanged leaving no one altered. This dynamic can also ruin a good party. Static minds are not open to learning, they are fighting for the comfort of completion, and stupid of that motivation.

The desire for a world where good and evil can be clearly distinguished, the desire for a moral position rather than inquiry, the desire to judge before one understands all violates the wisdom of uncertainty, ambiguity, and permanence.

Those early Greeks had a tolerance for the essential relativity of things human. They faced the foolishness of their desire for completion, set dogmas and permanence. They remind us that we can't even step into the same river twice.

Back to Kant, put simply. When the mind is able to take in as much as it can of the mass material of a given situation and organize it through thinking, the mind becomes most knowledgeable of that situation. But when the mind takes in only the material of a given situation that fits into one's belief system, the belief system gets reinforced, and knowledge of that situation is sacrificed. Reality does not care about what we believe.

CHAPTER FIVE

AUTHENTIC WISDOM VERSUS FALSE WISDOM

HOW DOES ONE discern the authentic from the false? Does it take special intelligence or specialized training? Or is it just that we all have different opinions and people have a right to their opinions? Are all opinions of equal value, just different? What's right and true for you is different than what's right and true for me. Is this just a case of embracing diversity? Is objectivity really another form of subjectivity?

Here again I think these early Greeks can help us out. To them wisdom had to do with three qualities that could largely be self-evident to the common person: Logos, Pathos, and Ethos.

LOGOS – We get the English word "logic" from this word. Logos means the love of truth, integrity, and authenticity. It also has to do with sound reasoning. Scientific research and proofs of reasoning lie at the heart of logos. A wise person is a person of truth.

Such a person embraces painful and embarrassing realities. They face inconvenient truths. They have a desire to learn and gain knowledge. They confront irrationalities, especially their own. Without truth there is no wisdom.

Today we are living in a period of political history where there is a reckless disregard for truth. Politicians lie. They have lied since time immemorial. Moises Naim in his book THE REVENGE OF POWER chronicles a history of spin and messaging, half-truths, and deceptions, and how they are as much a part of the democratic process as judicial review and periodic elections. But today a new word has been added to our dictionaries, post-truth.

Post-truth is different from simple political fibbing. It is not just about muddying the waters or rewriting history. It is about destroying the possibility of truth in public life. Collins English dictionary defines post-truth as "the disappearance of shared objective standards for truth."

It is a condition when facts and knowledge are not discernable from beliefs and opinions. The Yale historian, Timothy Snyder, points out that this is not just a personal fault of a given public figure, but a feature of the communications infrastructure of politics and power used by tyrants and dictators.

Philosopher Hannah Arendt, who barely survived the Holocaust after fleeing occupied Paris on a fake American visa explains, "The ideal subject of totalitarian rule is not the convinced Nazi or the convinced Communist, but people for whom the distinction between fact and fiction as well as true and false no longer exist."

Today the United States of America has become home to post-truth. It is everywhere in American life: the moon landing was a hoax, the Holocaust was made up, water-fluoridation is part of a mind-control experiment by the United Sates government, the HIV virus was developed as part of a U.S. biological weapon program, Obama was not born in America, or that John F Kennedy was assassinated by the CIA, were a part of disinformation that were easily dispelled.

We could prove that some of these originated from the Special Disinformation Office of the Soviets during the Cold War. But today things even more bizarre and fantastic live on because we are living in an age where there is an all-out attack on logos.

Recently Trump executives admitted passing on lies to Fox News who also knew they were lies but aired them anyway because that's what their subscribers needed to hear, and it was essential for their ratings. Both the executives and Fox News justified them as good business and have yet to indicate anything will change. Logos was sacrificed for more malevolent values. Recently these lies were about to be confronted in court. Fox News decided they would rather pay a quarter of a billion dollars than to tell the truth in court.

In the past, NEWS was always a losing enterprise financially. It was taken for granted it had to be that way. It was a responsibility not a business enterprise. That's all changed. Ratings and advertisers are the real motives too much of the time. As it was said, "They have eaten of the insane root that devores intellect and takes reason prisoner." (Macbeth)

Common people do not have to be victims of this. We can find truth and give integrity to logos. Here are three sources of reason available to a normal human (and there are many more than three of course):

1 – Develop your own reasoning capacity.

Descartes reminds us that the thinking self is the basis for everything human. One of most basic ways (for him the only certain way) to define a human being was to describe a human as a thinking being. His famous aphorism, "I think therefore I am" was at the heart of the enlightenment period. Human beings think. Even if they think badly, they still think. They cannot, not think.

Later, as mentioned earlier, Kant taught that we all are born with a capacity to organize our instinctual chaotic mind into thought. And since that chaotic instinctual mind is always active and infinite that process never ends but takes us to an ever higher ground, toward what he called "pure reason."

But here's the catch. That only happens when that process becomes purposeful. One has to be committed to do the work and Kant acknowledges that it is hard work. To think about your experiences, your education, your intuition (largely unconscious learning), your emotions, the things you read, the opinions of others, your own common sense, and forming your own reason out of all this will not happen in a lazy or faint mind. You will have to become a "free thinker" and not one of the herd or one who blindly follows the thinking of others.

More and more the general population avails themselves of psychotherapy. Good psychotherapy is all about growing the mind and confronting the obstacles that hinder that development.

Hannnah Arendt also had this insight from her research and experience with people under totalitarian rule. "It is easier to act under the conditions of tyranny than to think."

Erich Fromm in his book, THE FEAR OF FREEDOM teases out these same dynamics psychologically. It is easier to follow the thinking of authoritarian leaders than think for yourself.

Once you develop your own thinking capacities you will find an active subconscious learning emerge. There will be things you just know are true even though you can't prove it and you will know that something isn't right even though you can't prove it. This ring of truth and the ring of the false is not infallible but will turn out to be more accurate than not.

Discerning the difference between a teacher and a preacher is not all that difficult if you think about it. Giving power to one on a soap box, telling you how to think and being with someone who stimulates your own thinking is also not difficult to discern.

2- Practice critical thinking.

Critical thinking does not mean one should be critical of the thinking of others. It means to critique the thinking of others as well as our own. To critique is to look more deeply into something. Kant's CRITIQUE OF PURE REASON was certainly not criticizing reason but bringing a new and deeper thinking to it. Critical thinking is not "an argument against" but to "examine more deeply. "

But critical thinking can have a bit of a sting to it. Critique to Socrates meant asking questions about how one came to know what they were talking about. That's how he got the name of "gadfly" like the fly that irritated horses. "Gadfly" is the name Plato called Socrates for interfering with the status quo by asking upsetting questions usually directed at authorities.

Much of what goes down as knowledge is often nothing but repeated hearsay. To critique is to question. Critical thinking keeps us from rushing to conclusions and opens up ourselves to less answers and more questions. Critical thinking brings "the world of life" under a permanent light. It invites an appeal of thought and can lead to a radiant intelligence in some cases.

Critical thinking embraces complexities, "things are not as simple as you think." Critical thinking helps us to hear amid the din of easy quick answers that come faster than the questions. Critical thinking asks rhetorical questions that help us think about things more deeply, not questions to be answered. To answer a rhetorical question is to disrespect the question. Rhetorical questions provoke more questions than answers.

It has been said that the fool has an answer for every question while the wise have a question for every question.

3 – Consult experts

Plumbers know who the good plumbers are; electricians know who the good electricians are; pediatricians know who the good pediatricians are; researchers know who the good researchers are; airline pilots know who the good pilots are; violinists know who the good violinists are. We could go on and on, but you get the idea. It is stupid for a non-expert to evaluate an expert.

Philosopher Bertram Russell says this about academia, "The essence of academic freedom is that teachers should be chosen for their expertness in the subject they are to teach, and the judges of this expertness should be other experts. Whether a man is a good mathematician, or physicist, or chemist, can only be judged by other mathematicians, or physicists, or chemists."

A quack is a person who presents himself as one who has knowledge in areas where he has no expertise. Such a person is not aware of what he does not know. It is important to spot quacks.

If after a series of tests, a cardiologist says you need heart surgery, you might want to get a second or third opinion. But you do not go to your psychologist, or chiropractor, or those who went through heart surgery for their advice. You go to other cardiologists instead and your primary care physician will insist if he is not a quack.

The world is full of those who critique experts in areas where they have no expertise. We witnessed this most clearly with the Covid pandemic.

Dr. Anthony Fauci was among the most respected scientist and immunologist in the world by his peers and Donald Trump should be given credit for putting him in charge of the Covid crises. His work with Aids, saving millions of lives, not only earned him the Presidential Medal of Freedom, the highest civilian award in the U.S., but the awe of the scientific world.

Yet he had to suffer the stupidity of political leaders and the populace who felt they were in a position to critique his expertise that brought a vaccine in months that usually took years. Some political candidates promised to put him in jail if they got elected and his research was in constant conflict with the opinions of the President.

News sources voiced these critiques. It became heated. Unfortunately the critiques largely came from from quacks, rarely from the most esteemed scientists and experts in the field.

Most people are not aware of what scientific research is all about and the expertise and skills needed for such an endeavor. The world is full of anecdotal evidence. Advertisers use it, "I tried this product, and it took away my headache, or cleared up my skin, or gave me more energy."

Even in general conversations people offer a remedy that helped them with a certain medical issue, not knowing that anecdotal evidence is not scientific evidence. The correlations they put together are usually coincidences, but not always of course – at least it proves nothing scientifically.

Research takes very trained experts in the discipline of what counts as true research. How the research is set up, organized, finds its population, and is executed is very complex. The math involved takes skilled mathematicians.

When it came to Covid agencies like the Center for Disease Control and The National Institute of Allergy and Infectious Diseases had more expertise, more tools, more data of other research projects around the world, more funding than anywhere and yet were constantly demeaned by stupid politicians and the populace who had no idea of what they did not know.

In his book THE REVENGE OF POWER, Moises Naim focuses on how pseudoscience is used by autocrats to undermine democratic life in a new and frightening way. The lust for power has not changed, but the way autocrats go about it today has been transformed.

He writes, "Instead of attacking science head-on, lobbyists invest decades and huge amounts of resources to subvert it, financing experts to produce reports that have the look and feel of science but are no such thing, with the aim of creating the appearance of controversy

THE PSYCHOLOGY OF IGNORANCE

where none really exists. The basic move is always the same: appropriating the outward trappings of science to obscure real scientific findings."

How can the common man know the difference between pseudoscience and real science? Real scientific research demands peer review. Not all scientists are honest. Pseudoscience does not submit its work to other experts, to reputable scientific journals, or to established scientific organizations.

Think of the oil industry's effort to subvert climate science. For decades, giant oil companies spent freely in order to commission academic studies that found the threat from carbon pollution overblown. The papers these researchers produced looked and felt like real scientific papers. They purposefully mimic science.

Well documented articles along with books like, PRIVATE EMPIRE: EXXON MOBIL AN AMERICAN POWER, by Steve Coll and THE TRIUMP OF DOUBT: DARK MONEY AN THE SCIENCE OF DECEPTION by David Michaels, prove that these papers weren't science at all, but pseudoscience designed to cast doubt on the real thing.

Similar dynamics have played out in support of tobacco, sugary drinks, the mass prescription of opioids and the list goes on: junk science, dressed up to look like the real thing, is used again and again to justify the unjustifiable. It was when the Greeks lost their "logos" that they lost their democracy. Welcome to the Dark Ages which lasted for over a thousand years before democracies got another chance.

PATHOS – Pathos is the Greek word for suffering. It has to do with the ability to care about those who suffer. The literal translation of sympathy is "syn" (with) "pathy" (suffer) – to suffer with someone, to suffer together. Empathy is literally "em" (in) "pathy" (suffer). This is to be in the suffering of another. To put yourself in their shoes and feel it. Pathos is comprehending the needs, feelings, problems, and views of others as well as a sad concern for another's misfortune.

To these early Greeks logos was not enough. Wisdom also had to do with character. To be ignorant of character, to lack character was of great concern. A wise person had to come from the heart. Such a person could feel the pain of others and understand what it was like for them. A wise person is a feeling person and a compassionate person. Without compassion a person is nothing.

Even a child knows the difference between someone who understands them and someone who doesn't. Even a child knows the difference between a kind and loving person and someone who is not.

As mentioned earlier, during the 2016 campaign of Donald Trump's run for president a renowned group of mental health experts met at Yale University with great concern about the character and mental health of Donald Trump. Psychiatrists and psychologists like me are ethically bound to not diagnose a person we are not treating, especially public figures.

However, we also have a "Duty to Warn." If a patient of mine is planning to harm someone, I can no longer honor confidentiality. I must warn the proper agencies that protect children and adults alike. That was the conflict this Yale conference was about.

What the group concluded was that diagnosing Trump was not an issue. No one needed to diagnose him. He was out there publicly not only with his pathologies but also his character deficiencies.

"When you're a star, they let you do it. You can do anything…Grab 'em by the pussy…you can do anything." This was not said in the privacy of a psychotherapist's office but in a conversation with another guy.

"In addition to winning the Electoral College in a landslide, I won the popular vote if you deduct the millions of people who voted illegally" was not a delusion shared with a psychotherapist but on a stage in front of a crowd.

"I'm, like, a really smart person" – "It's hard for them to attack me on my looks, because I'm so good looking" – "I alone can fix it." – I'm speaking with myself, number one, because I have a very good brain...My primary consultant is myself" is his public discourse.

"Now the poor guy. You ought to see this guy" was a remark made while contorting his face and moving his arms and hands around awkwardly at a campaign rally in South Carolina, about journalist Serge Kovaleski, who has arthrogryposis, a congenital condition that can limit joint movement or lock limbs in place.

Like a teenager he mocked colleagues in a bullying way: lying Ted, little Mario, low energy Jeb, crooked Hillary, crazy Bernie, wacky, low life, loser Omarosa, Pocahontas referring to Elizabeth's family belief that they had an Indian heritage, slippery James Comey and more. He was proud that these names came to him instinctually.

"I hope Corrupt Hillary Clinton chooses Goofy Elizabeth Warren as her running mate. I will defeat them both." All these things reveal much about his character. Can you imagine a man like that becoming our President?

Can you imagine any public official saying he could commit murder on main street and the people would still worship him? Aren't all people turned off by the braggard? A kid who acted like that in my high school would need protection from a lot of other guys. But Trump used it to become President.

Trump was very complimentary about the most ruthless and brutal dictators in our contemporary world. They murdered, tortured, led mass killings of their own family and citizens – people who would love to destroy us as a nation – leaders who loved the terrorism of those who took down the twin towers in New York and would do worse for us if they could. He admired these powerful and authoritarian leaders, envied them.

Kim Jong-un: "You gotta give him credit...when his father died, he goes in, takes over the tough generals and he's the boss. It's incredible.

He wipes out the uncle, wipes out this one, that one. It's incredible."

Bashar al Assad: "I think in terms of leadership, he's getting an A and our president is not doing too well."

Saddam Hussein:" Okay, so he was a very bad guy. But you know what he did well? He killed terrorists. He did that so good! He didn't read them their rights. They didn't talk. You were a terrorist, it's over!"

Vladimir Putin: "If he says great things about me, I'm going to say great things about him. He's very much a leader...very strong control over his country...and look, he has an eighty-two-percent approval rating!"

He boasted that if he became President, he'd put Hillary Clinton in jail.

Trump benefited by being underestimated. If any other political candidate would have said any one of the above statements, it'd be all over. If a school principal said any one of the above statements he or she would be done. When most of us heard any one of those things we felt, "This time Trump is done." But time after time he survived and he was brushed off as irrelevant, "That's just Trump. No one takes him seriously. He could never win an election."

Pretty soon everyone just got used to it, like the frog who stays in water that gets hotter and hotter until it kills him.

But the Yale conference wasn't taking this lightly. They saw the danger of making this the new normal. They concluded that "The duty to warn" was more important than giving blind eye to the train wreck they saw coming in the name of not "diagnosing someone they were not treating." Trump was putting it all out there with pride, unrestrained.

The cheating, the lying, the narcissistic and psychopathic configurations all under a bright light. The scamming of Trump University charging students $42,000 a year for courses they could get online free and so called professors never available, his non-profit corporation as another scam to make money, his racist real estate ventures, his cheating small business out of money he owed them, because they could not afford to fight him legally were all public knowledge and dealt with by the legal system. The psychopathology behind this all was clearly revealed, especially to trained psychologists.

So, twenty seven Psychiatrists and Mental Health Experts wrote the book, THE DANGEROUS CASE OF DONALD TRUMP and sounded the alarm of the disaster of this man becoming the President of the United States.

Almost everything they predicted came true. The populace had ignored the warning. Trump's charisma and cultic heroism took over. Character didn't matter anymore. Pathos didn't matter anymore.

ETHOS – Ethos is the third ingredient the early Greek associated with wisdom. We get the English word "ethics" from this word. It is best translated "Justice." Without ethos (a love of justice), logos and pathos are compromised. Logos, pathos, and ethos are so intertwined that one cannot exist without the others. They operate as a whole. They form their own gestalt.

If we are living in a world where logos and pathos are slowly departing from the seat whence it directed the universe of values, distinguished good from evil, and endowed each thing with meaning, then ethos will meet the same fate.

Darwin verified that competition, not fairness, was at the heart of our animal self, our biological instinctual self. As beautiful as nature can be, it can be ever so cruel and downright evil. He wrote in his notebook, "Our descent, then, is the origin of our evil passions!! The devil under form of Baboon is our grandfather."

He said of the bees, "There can hardly be a doubt that our unmarried females would, like worker bees, think it a sacred duty to kill their brothers, and mothers would strive to kill their fertile daughters; and no one would think of interfering."

Religions that believed a benevolent god created nature, blamed it on humans who were born in the sin of their own doing.

Around 1882 Darwin talked about a human capacity for sympathy. Human also had social instincts, but it would involve REASON, "As man advances in civilization, and small tribes are united into larger communities, the simplest reason would tell each individual that he ought to extend his social instincts and sympathies to all the members of the same nation, though personally unknown to him. This point being once reached, there is only an artificial barrier to prevent his sympathies extending to the men of all nations and races."

In other words, man had to be more than his instincts and it involved ethos and reason. John Stuart Mill wrote, "If there are any marks at all of special design in creation, one of the things most evidently designed is that a large portion of all animals should pass their existence in tormenting and devouring other animals...If Nature and Man are both works of a Being of perfect goodness, that Being intended Nature as a scheme to be amended, not imitated by Man."

Thomas Henry Huxley chimed in, "The practice of that which is ethically best – what we call goodness or virtue – involves a course of conduct which, in all respects, is opposed to that which leads to success in the cosmic struggle for existence. In place of ruthless self-assertion, it demands self-restraint; in place of thrusting aside, or treading down, all competitors, it requires that the individual shall not merely respect, but shall help his fellows; its influence is directed, not so much to the survival of the fittest, as to the fitting of as many as possible to survive."

In the same spirit Samuel Smiles wrote in his 1859 book SELF HELP, "The greatest slave is not he who is ruled by a despot, great though that evil be, but he who is in the thrall of his own moral ignorance, selfishness, and vice."

Darwin made ethos the meaning of life. It was not in the belief in "the existence of a personal God or of a future existence with retribution or reward" but "in accordance with the verdict of all the wisest men that the highest satisfaction is derived from following certain impulses, namely the social instincts. If he acts for the good of others, he will receive the approbation of his fellow men and gain the love of those with whom he lives" which he describes as a great pleasure. But he adds that if his reason is in opposition to the opinion of other and he loses that satisfaction, "he will still have the solid satisfaction of knowing that he followed his inner most guide or conscience."

For years after my organized basketball days were over, I've been involved in pick-up basketball games in city parks, YMCAs, and recreational centers where I lived. These games have certain unwritten rules that all players know. They actually differ little from city to city.

In pick-up, three on three, half-court basketball, the offensive player getting a rebound can immediately put up a shot, but a defensive player getting a rebound must first take the ball behind the free throw line before that player or his teammates can shoot. The player who feels he was fouled gets to call the foul. The team who scores gets to take the ball out again, but only when a defensive player passes the ball to them. How players waiting to play get on the court and who gets to stay on the court, are part of the unwritten list that goes on.

Of course, there are arguments at times, but players by-in- large all know and keep these rules. It's not "cool" to break them. It only shows how amateur one is if he doesn't know the rules, much less breaks them. Any player breaking them will soon be ostracized by the group.

In organized basketball (institutionalized basketball) the guard rails change. There, the referees, not the players, enforce the rules. But even if you can get away with playing dirty (getting away with stuff when the refs aren't looking), you pay a price with your peers. It's not "cool" to break the unwritten rules and the player that does loses the respect of other players, even his teammates. He will never be considered a great player no matter how talented he is.

The same is true in politics. There are unwritten rules and keepers of the guard rails. In all facets of society: family, community, business, educational institutions etc., unwritten rules loom large. In HOW DEMOCRACIES DIE, Harvard University professors of government, Steven Levitsky and Daniel Ziblatt, research how democracies die from 1930s Europe to contemporary Hungry, Turkey, Venezuela, to today's threat in America. They write, "Democracy no longer ends with a bang, in a revolutionary or military coup, but with a whimper…the gradual erosion of long-standing political norms.

The unwritten rules are vital "because of the gaps and ambiguities inherent in all legal systems, we cannot rely on constitutions alone to safeguard democracy against would-be authoritarians". The justice department cannot save us alone. There is always the spirit of the law that must rule. The spirit of ethos must dominate. The literal interpretation of laws can be quite unjust at times.

It is professional sports like Major League Baseball, the National Basketball Association, and the National Football League, that are shining examples of what we wish politics would be. Most likely that is a major factor why they are popular and a constructive national pastime – also a healthy example of ethos.

Today the referees and umpires, those who maintain the guardrails of those sports, are committed to making the right call. They cannot be corrupted. The best and most talented at that task get to work the Super Bowl, the World Series, and the NBA final. They obtain their job because they proved they were fit for such work. They came through the ranks.

On close calls they often consult the other officials for their take (peer review), they want to get it right. Any close call can be challenged and under the bright light of a slow motion camera for all the fans to see. The official is only too glad for this help and gladly reverses his call when needed.

There are guard rails to protect players from getting hurt. Flagrant fouls, unnecessary roughness, bean balls can all get a player ejected. Players are also protected from psychological abuse. Unsportsmanship-conduct is not tolerated. Taunting another player after getting the best of him is penalized.

The New Orleans Saints was accused of "Bounty Gate" paying players bounties for injuring star players of opposing teams during the 2009-2011 football season. The penalties were massive. The organization was fined $500,000 and had to forfeit their second-round draft choices in 2012 and 2013. It was the first time a head coach was suspended. A number of other coaches were suspended along with a mass of players. It decimated their football team for some time.

Baseball teams have faced sanctions for using technology to steal signs of opposing teams. Spousal abuse has kept star players from playing. Yes, there are "bad apples," but they are quickly weaned out.

One of the valued awards in football (and other sports have their own) is the Walter Payton Humanitarian Award given to the athlete who has contributed the most to his community. Athletes give of themselves to the needs of their communities. It's one of the many unwritten values.

Every fan in their own living room witnesses opposing players hugging each other after intense hard fought games. They play and fight as enemies, but when the game is over the ethos is well in place. Each of these major sport teams have an all-star game (usually mid-season) where they take a break, and the best players get to play on the same team with each other. The comradery and good-will is a joy to watch.

Ironically, it is the athletes not the politicians that are keeping ethos alive and serve as a model as to what can and should be for politicians. Those basic civic and humane unwritten values and attitudes are long gone in today's political arena. No team owner would ever think of asking for loyalty from a referee.

The "Shining City on the Hill," the phrase used by politicians as a premonition of America's greatness is now in the hands of other institutions. Bill Maher on his show (2/17/23) presents numerous movies where the leading stars hated each other and yet got it done and asks why politicians can't do this. How did it get this way?

Levitsky and Ziblatt take on that question in their book HOW DEMOCRACIS FAIL. "Two norms stand out as fundamental to a functioning democracy: mutual toleration and institutional forbearance."

What does mutual tolerance look like to these men? "Mutual tolerance refers to the idea that as long as our rivals play by constitutional rules, we accept that they have an equal right to exist, compete for power and govern. We may disagree with, and even strongly dislike, our rivals, but we nevertheless accept them as legitimate. This means recognizing that our political rivals are decent, patriotic, law-abiding citizens that love our country."

What about institutional forbearance? "Forbearance means patient self-control; restraint and tolerance, or the action of restraining from exercising a legal right. For our purposes, institutional forbearance can be thought of as avoiding actions that, while respecting the letter of the law, obviously violate its spirit…Without forbearance, checks and balances give way to deadlock and dysfunction."

They point out that norm breaking has always existed in American politics and America's democratic institutions were challenged on several occasions during the twentieth century, but each of these challenges from Roosevelt's unprecedented concentration of executive power during the great depression and World War II, to Eisenhower's tolerance of McCarthyism, to Nixon's criminal assault on democratic institutions, the guardrails held. Each of these challenges were effectively contained. Politicians from both parties along with society as a whole pushed back against these violations.

The concern of HOW DEMOCRACIES DIE is how that all changed, not just with Trump. It started in 1979 and never got contained. Ever since, the guardrails have become more and more vulnerable. Trump just doubled down and took advantage of this dynamic.

In June 1979 Newt Gingrich arrived in Washington with a vision of politics as warfare which was at odds with that of the Republican leadership. HOW DEMOCRACIES DIE states, "House Minority Leader Bob Michel, an amiable figure who carpooled to Illinois for congressional recesses with his Democratic colleague Dan Rostenkowski, was committed to abiding by established norms of civility and bipartisan cooperation. Gingrich rejected this approach as too soft." Winning a Republican majority, Gingrich believed, would require playing a harder form of politics.

In June of his 1978 campaign, Gingrich found a hungry audience for a cutthroat vision of politics. He warned young Republicans to stop using "Boy Scout words, which would be great around a campfire, but lousy in politics."

Gingrich told them, "You're fighting a war. It is a war for power...This party does not need another generation of cautious, prudent, careful, bland irrelevant quasi-leaders...What we really need are people who are willing to stand up in a slugfest."

What came out of Gingrich's mouth was never heard before from either side. It was so far over the top that the shock factor rendered the opposition frozen for years. He described his congressional opponents as "corrupt" and "sick," comparing them to Mussolini.

HOW DEMOCRACIES DIE says by the early 1990s, "Gingrich and his team distributed memos to Republican candidates instructing them to use certain negative words to describe Democrats, including pathetic, sick, bizarre, betray, antiflag, antifamily, and traitors." The seismic shift was taking hold in American politics. Ethos was being ridiculed.

While Gingrich may have led the initial assault on mutual tolerance and forbearance, the descent into politics of warfare only accelerated after he left congress in 1999. The real power fell into the hands of House Majority Leader Tom Delay, nicknamed "the hammer."

DeLay shared, if not accelerated Gingrich's partisan ruthlessness. In fear that Bush might be more a "uniter" than a "divider" mellowed by Gore's conceding the Presidency to him, HOW DEMOCRACIES DIE continues, "Delay gave the president-elect a reality check, reportedly telling him, 'We don't work with Democrats. There'll be none of that uniter-divider stuff.' Senate Democrats also began to stray from the norm of forbearance."

Under Bush America went into an unjust war with little resistance from oversight referees and for the first time in American history, torturing prisoners was justified. And the list goes on. It's well documented and worth reading about.

By the time Trump arrived the stage was set. Trump was not elected in spite of his lack of ethos, but because of it.

If Obama brought back some spirit of ethos, Trump made sure to destroy it. Obama was characterized as, the first anti-American president, someone who should go back to Africa where he came from, he's not one of us, he wasn't even born in America, he doesn't love America, he wants to destroy our nation, someone who launched his political career in the living room of a domestic terrorist and the list goes on as the crowds cheered.

Though McCain selected a ruthless running mate in Sarah Palin, McCain did not employ such rhetoric. He brought ethos back in the peaceful transfer of power. On election night there was this ray of hope for a return of a more civilized brand of politics. He delivered a gracious concession speech in which he described Obama as a good man who loved his country and wished him "Godspeed."

Not to be, the crowd booed loudly, forcing McCain to calm them down. Trump would be the man they were looking for. The most important policy for Republicans until the next election was declared by the Senate Minority Leader Mitch McConnell, "The single most important thing we want to achieve in the Senate is for President Obama to be a one-term President." However, they would have to wait another eight years for their man to appear.

I need not go into any more detail of how Trump attacked ethos. He attacked ethos in the same way he attacked logos and pathos. Are we really to the point that when a president gives his state of the union address, we should expect heckling from opposing congressmen or congresswomen?

Timothy Snyder presented the strategies by which elected conscience-less, authoritarians seek to consolidate power. There are three key strategies: capturing the referees, sidelining key players, and rewriting the rules to tilt the playing field against opponents. Trump attempted all three of these strategies.

Does character matter? Abraham Lincoln said that if you want to know the character of a man, give him power. The question for all of us is, "Does character matter for me, does character matter for you?" We are the ones who vote these people in or out.

"Character" has to go through a developmental process. The former Harvard University professor, Lawrence Kohlberg studied this development from childhood to maturity. He came up with six stages of moral development. He believed that everyone goes through each stage in the same order, but not all go through all the stages:

Stage one – "I do the right thing because if I don't, I will get punished."

Stage two – "I do the right thing because I will be rewarded, and other people will help me."

Stage three – "I do the right thing because people important to my life will be pleased and think well of me."

Stage four – "I do the right thing because I have a role in society and laws make life fair and orderly."

Stage five – "I do the right thing because it contributes to the social well-being and that each member of society has an obligation to every other member."

Stage six – "I do the right thing because of my personal conscience, and I don't want to violate myself."

Kohlberg saw these as stages, but I think we can also think of them as to what motivates us in any given situation. The key of course is to be in touch with our true motives and have the courage to face our virtuous and not so virtuous self that continues to alternate throughout a lifetime.

We need to go beyond Kohlberg to the fact that perhaps everything we do is self-serving in some way or other. This idea goes as far back as Martin Luther, who said a saint is someone who understands that everything he does is egotistical.

Love of self is not all that bad. The New Testament claims Jesus took self-love for granted when he said that the hundreds of laws in the Old Testament could be fulfilled by loving God and your neighbor as much as you love yourself.

Jesus also acknowledged that humans have a basic bias toward self; that the lack self-awareness was one obvious human delusion, "He that is without sin among you cast the first stone...thou hypocrite, first cast out the beam out of thine own eye before you cast out the sliver in your thy brother's eye."

Buddha said in plain language, "The fault of others is easily perceived, but that of one's self is difficult to perceive."

Instinctually we are naturally skewed in our perspective of ourselves.

Back to where we began. Those early Greeks believed that wisdom had to do with self-awareness. The self-aware person will always possess a deeper wisdom than an expert lacking self-awareness. "Know Thyself" and "The Unexamined life is not worth living" are all about self-awareness. Ignorance, knowing what you do not know, is a part of that self-awareness.

The main characteristic of a person of character is not one's record around doing the right and virtuous thing. It is "the examined life." The main characteristic is being aware of one's virtuous failures and desire to change and fix it.

One can grow in self-awareness and work with his or her ignorance, but one can't grow in stupidity. A self-aware person has many advantages. Self-knowledge not only allows us to better understand ourselves, but also others and life in general. Self-knowledge allows one to have keener insights and wisdom into social and political life. It doesn't take a gifted mind to recognize a person with self-awareness and a person who lacks it. It is one of those things that become obvious to an insightful mind.

Self-awareness also has a therapeutic value. It adds to self-esteem, personal power, and a more confident and solid self, because the self-aware person is grounded in himself or herself, in the authenticity of one's own personal truth, knowing the difference between a "true self" and a "false self."

The self-aware person carries a certain comfort internally and is less dependent on others for narcissistic supplies and can be less injured by the slings and arrows of others. Such a person is aware of the many conflicts and obstacles that can derail this process. Self-awareness has to be earned and nurtured. It is most human and humane. It has an equality to it. The gifted have no advantage in this arena.

James Madison wrote, "If men were angles, no government would be necessary." In other words, our founders saw government as the agency to preserve logos, pathos, and ethos because there will be times when the citizenry will lose sight of what it means to be a good citizen.

We should be alarmed when the government no longer plays that role. We should also be alarmed when as citizens we no longer feel this responsibility to each other, where truth, compassion, and fairness can be sacrificed when it doesn't serve our own purposes, when we become blind to our own ignorance.

Just know! There was a time when an education involved more than gaining information and expertise. The kind of person we were becoming mattered.